★★★ F-14 TOMCATS

BY **JACK DAVID**

BELLWETHER MEDIA · MINNEAPOLIS, MN

Are you ready to take it to the extreme?
Torque books thrust you into the action-packed
world of sports, vehicles, and adventure. These books
may include dirt, smoke, fire, and dangerous stunts.
WARNING: read at your own risk.

Library of Congress Cataloging-in-Publication Data

David, Jack, 1968-
  F-14 Tomcats / by Jack David.
     p. cm. — (Torque: military machines)
  Includes bibliographical references and index.
  Summary: "Amazing photography and engaging information explain the technologies and
capabilities of the F-14 Tomcats. Intended for students in grades 3 through 7"—Provided by
publisher.
  ISBN-13: 978-1-60014-202-4 (hardcover : alk. paper)
  ISBN-10: 1-60014-202-8 (hardcover : alk. paper)
  1. Tomcat (Jet fighter plane)—Juvenile literature. I. Title.

  UG1242.F5.D3465 2008
  623.74'64—dc22   2008019863

This edition first published in 2009 by Bellwether Media.

The photographs in this book are reproduced through the courtesy of the United States Department of
Defense.

Printed in the United States of America.

CONTENTS

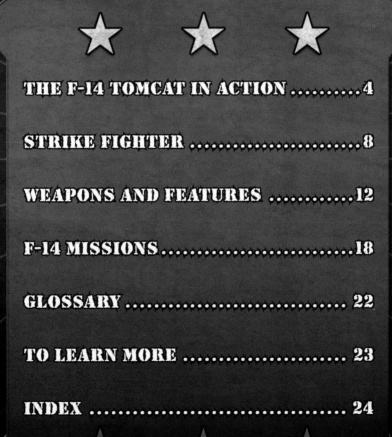

THE F-14 TOMCAT IN ACTION 4

STRIKE FIGHTER 8

WEAPONS AND FEATURES 12

F-14 MISSIONS.............................18

GLOSSARY 22

TO LEARN MORE 23

INDEX 24

THE F-14 TOMCAT IN ACTION

Two F-14 Tomcats streak across the sky. Their **mission** is to bomb an enemy base. As they reach the target, two enemy fighter planes appear.

The F-14 pilots fire two AIM-9 Sidewinder **missiles**. The powerful missiles smash into the enemy planes. The planes blow up in a cloud of smoke.

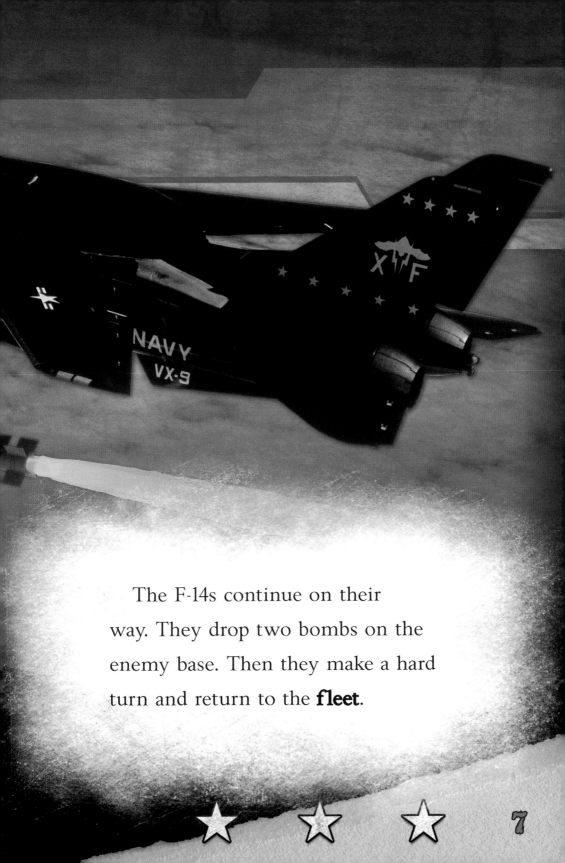

The F-14s continue on their way. They drop two bombs on the enemy base. Then they make a hard turn and return to the **fleet**.

STRIKE FIGHTER

The F-14 Tomcat was the United States Navy's best **strike fighter** for more than 30 years. The Navy used it to fight enemy aircraft, bomb targets on land and sea, and gather **intelligence** about the enemy. The twin-engine plane was fast, easy to handle, and powerful.

★ **FAST FACT** ★

The Navy built the F-14 to replace another very successful fighter, the F-4 Phantom.

The F-14 made its first flight in 1970. Its ability to take off from and land on **aircraft carriers** made it perfect for the Navy. Its main job was fleet defense. In 2006, the Navy retired the Tomcat. The F/A-18E/F Super Hornet replaced it as the Navy's main fleet protector.

The F-14 had "swept" wings. The wings could partly "sweep in" so that they didn't use too much space on an aircraft carrier. They "swept out" when the F-14 was ready to take off.

WEAPONS AND FEATURES

The F-14 was built for battle. Its main weapon was an M61 Vulcan machine gun that could fire as many as 6,000 rounds per minute.

13

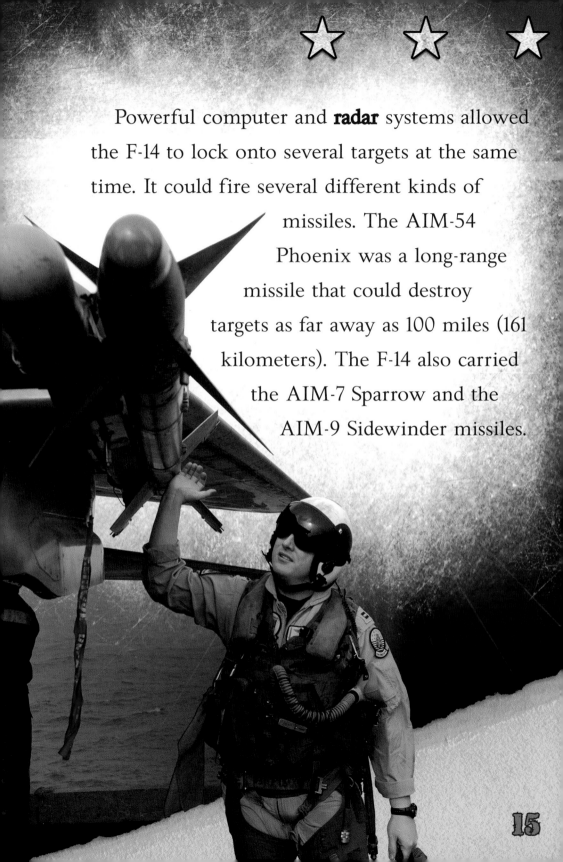

Powerful computer and **radar** systems allowed the F-14 to lock onto several targets at the same time. It could fire several different kinds of missiles. The AIM-54 Phoenix was a long-range missile that could destroy targets as far away as 100 miles (161 kilometers). The F-14 also carried the AIM-7 Sparrow and the AIM-9 Sidewinder missiles.

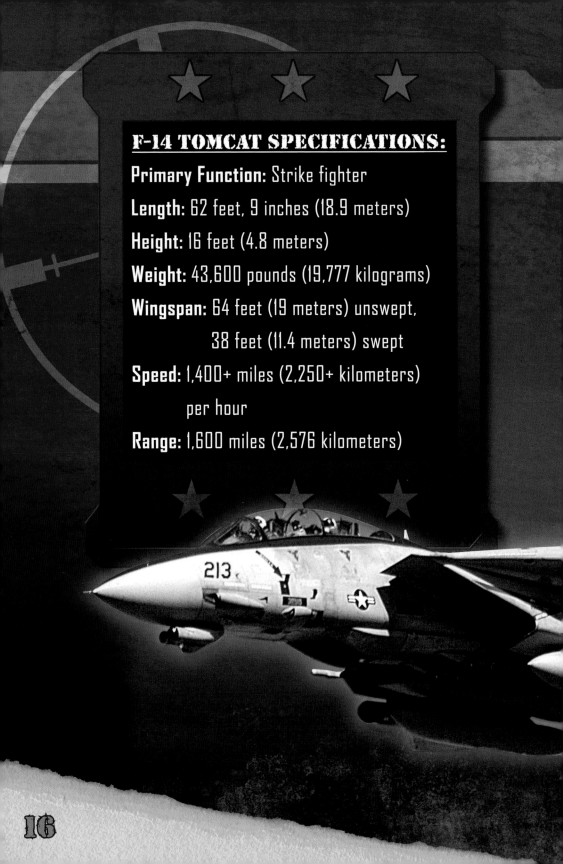

F-14 TOMCAT SPECIFICATIONS:

Primary Function: Strike fighter

Length: 62 feet, 9 inches (18.9 meters)

Height: 16 feet (4.8 meters)

Weight: 43,600 pounds (19,777 kilograms)

Wingspan: 64 feet (19 meters) unswept,
38 feet (11.4 meters) swept

Speed: 1,400+ miles (2,250+ kilometers)
per hour

Range: 1,600 miles (2,576 kilometers)

The F-14 could also destroy ground targets. The 2,000-pound MK-84 bomb could level entire buildings. **Laser-guided bombs (LGBs)** and air-to-ground missiles could lock onto their targets. Cluster bombs could destroy enemy tanks. On board the F-14 there was a weapon for almost any purpose.

F-14 MISSIONS

Every F-14 had a crew of two Navy officers. The pilot flew the plane and operated many of the weapons. The **radar intercept officer (RIO)** helped with the weapons and navigation. Groups of F-14s flew together in **formations**.

★ **FAST FACT** ★

The F-14 had hardpoints under its wings. Weapons were attached to these hardpoints.

The Navy used the F-14 for a variety
of missions. It patrolled the air around
a fleet. It performed quick strikes on
enemy targets in the air or on the
ground. It flew **reconnaissance** missions
to learn about an enemy. It was a
valuable plane that served the U.S. Navy
well for more than 30 years.

GLOSSARY

aircraft carrier—a huge Navy ship from which airplanes can take off and land

fleet—a large group of ships

formation—the pattern in which a group of planes fly

intelligence—information about an enemy

laser-guided bomb (LGB)—an explosive that locks onto a target that has been marked with a laser

missile—an explosive launched at targets on the ground or in the air

mission—a military task

radar—a sensor system that uses radio waves to locate objects

radar intercept officer (RIO)—the crew member of an F-14 who helps the pilot navigate, prepare weapons, and find targets

reconnaissance—secret observation

strike fighter—a military airplane designed to carry out attacks on enemies on the ground or in the air

TO LEARN MORE

AT THE LIBRARY

David, Jack. *United States Navy.* Minneapolis, Minn.: Bellwether, 2008.

Gardner, Adrian. *The F-14 Tomcat.* New York: Rosen, 2003.

Green, Michael and Gladys. *Carrier-Based Jet Fighters: The F-14 Tomcats.* Mankato, Minn.: Capstone, 2007.

ON THE WEB

Learning more about military machines is as easy as 1, 2, 3.

1. Go to www.factsurfer.com

2. Enter "military machines" into search box.

3. Click the "Surf" button and you will see a list of related web sites.

With factsurfer.com, finding more information is just a click away.

INDEX

1970, 10
2006, 10
aircraft carriers, 10, 11
bombs, 7, 17
cluster bombs, 17
F-4 Phantom, 9
F/A-18E/F Super
    Hornet, 10
fleet, 7, 10, 21
formations, 18
hardpoints, 19
intelligence, 8
laser-guided bombs
    (LGBs), 17
M61 Vulcan, 12
missiles, 6, 15, 17
missions, 4, 21
navigation, 18
officers, 18

pilot, 18
radar, 15
radar intercept officer
    (RIO), 18
reconnaissance, 21
strike fighter, 8
swept wings, 11
United States Navy, 8, 9,
    10, 21